Building Wealth Through Agriculture

The New Frontier of Investments

Table of Contents

Chapter 1. Introduction

In recent years, a previously overlooked sector has been quietly blooming as the new frontier in investments - agriculture. This Special Report, "Building Wealth Through Agriculture: The New Frontier of Investments," meticulously uncovers how everyday investors and seasoned venture capitalists are turning to agriculture as a potent, viable, and sustainable wealth-building option. It's not just about sowing seeds and reaping harvests anymore; it's about strategic investments, technological advancements, sustainability, and above all, financial prosperity. Designed to thoroughly inform without overwhelming, this report brilliantly merges technical depth with accessible insights, making it ideal for both novice and expert investors. So embark on this empowering journey with us as we cultivate your investment portfolio's growth, just as a skillful farmer nurtures their crops. Invest in this Special Report to get groundbreaking strategies and begin your lucrative journey in the verdant fields of agriculture.

Chapter 2. The Roots of Agricultural Investment

To fully understand the emergence and appeal of agricultural investments, one must first delve into the origins or, aptly termed, the roots of agricultural investment. Any story of prosperity told without acknowledging its beginnings will paint an inauthentic picture. Appreciating the evolution of agricultural investment from its rudimentary origins to its sophisticated, technology-driven present status helps underscore its future potential.

2.1. Early Investing Paradigms

Before industrialization, the predominant form of wealth was land ownership. Agricultural land, in particular, was the cornerstone of socioeconomic stability, enabling self-sufficiency and providing potential surplus for trade or sale. As societies evolved, the accumulation of agricultural land was often equated with wealth, power, and prosperity. As today's investors revisit this time-tested principle, the focus has shifted from outright ownership of arable land to long-term investment in multifaceted agricultural enterprises.

2.2. The Emergence of Agricultural Commodities

The industrial revolution and increasing global trade gave rise to agricultural commodities as profitable investment avenues. Commodities like wheat, cotton, and later soybeans, corns, became the backbone of local economies and international trade. Come the 20th century, these agricultural commodities began trading on the futures market, presenting a new kind of risk-reward investment opportunity.

Investing in commodities via futures contracts allowed individuals and institutions an avenue to gain exposure to agriculture without the necessity of physical ownership or the difficulties of managing farmlands. The resultant market liquidity and trading volume made agricultural commodities an enticing choice for speculators and investors alike.

2.3. Institutional and Private Investments

Moving into the latter half of the 20th century, a significant development was the emergence of institutional investments in agriculture. Large entities, such as pension funds and private equity firms, identified the attractive qualities of agriculture — tangible assets, stable returns, and inflation hedge — and began acquiring significant stakes in farmland and agribusinesses internationally.

Simultaneously, private investments began flowing into agricultural technology companies, driven by the promise of disruptive innovation. These ranged from advancements in genetically modified organisms (GMOs) and precision farming to novel food production methods like vertical farming. As a result, agriculture began to move away from being a purely commodity and land-driven investment to one involving technology and entrepreneurial ventures.

2.4. Emergence of AgriTech

The 21st century has witnessed an exponential surge in technological development, particularly in the agricultural sector. This has set the stage for the emergence of AgriTech — a term used to describe innovations designed to enhance crop yield, improve resource efficiency, and reduce environmental impact.

Companies are developing groundbreaking technologies such as artificial intelligence (AI) driven farm management systems, satellite imagery for crop monitoring, and data analytics for supply chain optimization. Investors now have the opportunity to invest in these companies, essentially betting on the future of farming. These investments provide not only financial returns but also contribute to the overall betterment of the sector and society at large.

2.5. Impact of Global Issues

Key global issues such as population growth, climate change, and food security are shaping current agricultural investing trends. Population growth demands an increase in food production, climate change necessitates the development of resilient agricultural practices, and the issue of food security underscores the need for local, sustainable farming solutions.

These challenges have led to the rise of impact investing in agriculture, where the dual goals are financial returns and making measurable, positive impacts on these global issues. This blend of purpose and profit has resonated strongly with the current generation of investors.

In retrospect, the roots of agricultural investment stem from traditional land ownership centers and commodity trading, evolving into complex, technology-focused and impact-driven practices. Understanding this path helps investors appreciate the transformative journey of agriculture. As they say, to predict the future, one must first explore the past. The history of agricultural investment suggests a future filled with growth opportunities, purpose-driven innovation, and sustainable wealth creation. This new frontier of investment, with its deep roots and vast potential, awaits the investors willing to till its fertile ground.

Chapter 3. Understanding Agri-business: The Key Aspects

This chapter will begin with a description of what agriculture and agri-business entail. Agriculture refers to the process of producing food, feed, fiber, and many other desired products by the systematic raising of plants and animals. Agri-business, on the other hand, is the business of agricultural production. It involves all the steps required to send an agricultural good to market: production, processing, and distribution. It's an integral part of the agriculture industry that tends to be more profitable and reliable.

3.1. The Modern Agri-business Landscape

Agri-business has evolved immensely from the time when farming was only about a sickle, plow, and some healthy livestock. Modern farming practices use cutting-edge technology like hydroponics, GPS automated tractors, soil analysis bots, drone surveillance, and much more. Many agri-businesses have consolidated into large, corporate entities that manage vast tracts of land across several continents. The modern agricultural landscape encompasses everything from small-scale, organic growers serving local communities to vast agricultural conglomerates serving global markets with a variety of products.

Concurrently, a notable trend is the steady increase in the importance of agri-tech, improvement in farming techniques using technology, including precision farming, automation and robotics, soil and crop technology, farming data and software, and bioengineering. In turn, these advancements have made farming more efficient, cost-effective, and sustainable.

3.2. Role of Agri-business in the Economy

Agri-business plays an essential role in driving the world economy and manipulating the political landscape. The sector contributes significantly to export revenues in numerous countries, creates employment opportunities, provides a raw material base for numerous industries, and ensures food security at a global level. Additionally, a thriving agri-business sector can lead to rural development and poverty reduction, as it forms the economic backbone of many developing regions across the world.

Recent economic trends have also seen the rise of great interest in agri-business investments by both institutional and individual investors. These include areas like farmland ownership, technology solutions for agriculture, organic farming, vertical farming, and food processing, among others. The next sections will delve deeper into the opportunities and challenges that face investors in this ever-evolving domain.

3.3. Investment in Agri-business

Investing in agri-business can be an effective way to diversify your investment portfolio. Farmland, in particular, is a tangible asset that can provide a hedge against inflation. Plus, the overall demand for food and other agricultural products is steady and rising, given the consistent increase in global population and income levels.

However, it's crucial to know specific risks, such as unpredictable weather, commodity price volatility, land valuation, and political risks, among others. Also, the agri-business sector requires in-depth knowledge about farming practices, global market trends, regulatory policies, and new technologies.

Agriculture-focused mutual funds or exchange-traded funds (ETFs), and direct investments in farmland or agri-tech startups, are becoming increasingly popular. We shall delve into these investment types in later sections of this report.

3.4. Technological Advancements in Agri-business

From drone technology to Big Data, technology is reshaping the agriculture sector. These technologies increase agricultural productivity while reducing the environmental footprint. For example, precision farming technologies help in optimizing the inputs used for farming, such as water and fertilizers, thereby reducing the environmental impact while increasing productivity.

Farm management software and mobile apps have brought the convivence of managing the farms, overseeing crop growth, analyzing the soil, and maintaining the farm books in the palm of a hand. Genetic technologies have made it possible to develop crops with higher nutritional values, resilience to disease, and multiple other beneficial traits.

The latest trend is the use of Artificial Intelligence (AI) and machine learning in farming. These technologies can predict weather patterns, monitor crop health, and provide valuable data to farmers to optimize their farming strategy.

3.5. Sustainability in Agri-business

Given the increasing concerns over climate change and environmental degradation, sustainable methods of farming and agri-business practices have taken center stage. This includes practices such as organic farming, agroforestry, conservation tillage, and sustainable packaging in the food processing industry.

Agri-businesses implementing sustainable practices have the

potential to access new markets, enhance their reputation, and contribute to regional environmental goals. Furthermore, numerous investors are integrating Environmental, Social, and Governance (ESG) aspects into their investment decisions, placing sustainable agri-businesses at a significant advantage.

The future of agri-business appears to rest heavily on technological advancements, better farming techniques, and sustainable practices. Thus, investment in these areas is likely to continue to grow and retain its significance in the worldwide economic landscape. As an investor, understanding how these factors interact and what trends are set to shape the sector will be key to success.

In this rapidly evolving and promising landscape, the agri-business sector looks set to offer a host of rewarding investment opportunities, as long as one navigates the risks and challenges with an informed and strategic approach. The secrets of the trade lie in understanding this complex business, keeping updated with technological advancements, and staying committed to sustainability. Agri-business may very well be the new frontier for both wealth creation and environmental sustainability, fulfilling both economic and social targets in one fell swoop.

Investing in agri-business requires a deep understanding of the sector, a good grasp of the global market, and sensitivity towards sustainability. With the right approach, it promises high returns, coupled with an opportunity to contribute to global food security and sustainability.

Chapter 4. The Symbiosis of Finance and Farming

In examining the symbiotic relationship between finance and farming, it's essential first to delve into the definition of a symbiotic relationship - an interaction between two distinct entities that yields mutual benefits. Thus, when considering financing and farming, the connection is characterized by financial institutions providing agricultural businesses and farmers with the capital they need to invest in their operations. On the flip side, the farming operations provide financial institutions with returns on their investment, thus completing the mutual exchange.

4.1. Evolution of the Financial-Farming Relationship

The financial-farming relationship isn't a novel concept. However, the evolving nature of both industries, coupled with technological advancements, has significantly changed how this relationship looks. In the past, farmers were largely reliant on their own wealth, family funding, or loans from local banks for their financial means. Ventures into agriculture were mainly small-scale, characterized by subsistence farming rather than extensive commercial operations.

Today, it's quite different - investors and financial institutions, recognising the scalability and potential profitability of agriculture, are keen on making strategic investments in the sector. Consequently, the farming industry has seen a surge in the implementation of cutting-edge technology, including specifically designed software applications and innovative farming equipment, all aimed at enhancing production outcomes and consequently, profit margins.

4.2. The Farm's Financial Lifeline

The finance part of the symbiosis breathes life into the agriculture sector, providing the much-needed capital for various uses.

1. To begin with, financial initiatives offer startup capital to new farmers or those looking to expand their existing operations. This capital is vital for acquiring farmland, infrastructure and requisite tools necessary for modern-age farming.

2. Secondly, financial backing avails funds for machinery and equipment - the backbone of productivity in agriculture. Farmers need modern, efficient machines to stay competitive. Financing provides just that - ensuring farmers have access to the best tools of the trade.

3. Thirdly, funds are also provided for research and development efforts. These efforts are crucial in driving the adoption of sustainable and tech-oriented farming practices, which are both beneficial for the environment and for farms' productivity levels.

4.3. The Driving Forces of Farm Finance

While private investors and financial institutions are the dominant sources of funding in the farming field, there are also other notable contributors including the government and crowdfunding initiatives. Each one brings unique advantages:

1. Private investors and financial institutions are the heavyweights in farming finance. Their already established reputation and deep pockets make them valuable contributors to the sector. They offer flexible loan agreements but are mostly inclined towards large scale ventures due to their preference for more significant returns.

2. Government initiatives, on the other hand, offer secure and often low-interest loans to farmers. They are driven by the desire to boost domestic food production or encourage certain farming practices. However, these loans are often tied to stringent terms and conditions that farmers must meet.

3. Crowdfunding initiatives are the new entrants in this domain, largely driven by digital technology. They offer an inclusive platform for all to contribute, whether in small or large amounts. They tend to be more flexible and are particularly attractive to small scale farmers.

4.4. The Yield of Finance Farming

Financial farming symbiosis promises returns for both parties involved. For the farming initiatives, the immediate return is capital, which is used to upgrade operations, leading to improved productivity and consequently, larger revenue streams. Passive farmers, those who invest in farmland without actively managing it, are also able to get regular returns from their investment.

On the other hand, for the financial institutions, the return on investment is realised in the form of interest from loans or profits from investment initiatives. The growth potential in the agricultural sector also ensures that these investments are secured, promising even further returns in the future as farming operations expand, innovate, and become more profitable.

4.5. Enriching Symbiosis through Technology

Technology is the enabler that has not only redefined modern farming but has also fortified the bond between farming and finance.

1. Agriculture technologies, also known as Agritech, have made it

easier for farmers to maximize production while optimizing costs, attracting financiers as the profit margins look attractive. Agritech players provide farmers with the tools and knowledge needed to cultivate crops more efficiently and sustainably, using fewer natural resources, and reducing environmental impact.

2. Financial technology, or Fintech, has equally played a significant role in agriculture. Fintech has redefined traditional financial services and made them more accessible. Through mobile banking, online platforms, and alternative lending options, Fintech brings financial services closer to farmers, thus fostering the relationship.

4.6. Nurturing the Symbiosis

For this symbiosis to be truly impactful and sustainable, it's important that financial institutions invest not just capital, but also time and resources, to understand the dynamics and challenges of agriculture. Continuous dialogue and partnerships between financial institutions and farmers are of the essence.

Providing financial literacy training to farmers to handle credit responsibly and employ solid financial management practices is essential. Stakeholders should also work together to create insurance schemes that protect both lenders and farmers from potential risks associated with farming, such as crop failure due to undesirable weather conditions.

It's all about nurturing a symbiotic relationship that grows along with the industry it supports. As both finance and farming continue their relentless march into the future, they will undoubtedly remain intertwined in a way that makes both sectors stronger, sustainable, and ultimately more successful. The symbiosis of finance and farming is a compelling narrative of growth – one that aids economic development and sustains livelihoods. This relationship, if nurtured well, has the potential to not just transform the future of agriculture, but also the global economic landscape.

Chapter 5. Investment Options in the Agricultural Sector

When considering investment in the agricultural sector, one is presented with a cornucopia of potential avenues, each characterized by its own unique range of opportunities and challenges. This sector is diversifying and expanding into niches that were practically nonexistent a generation ago.

5.1. Traditional Crop Farming

Historically, farming was the cornerstone of agriculture investment. Traditional crops include grains such as wheat, corn, and rice, along with fruits, vegetables, and nuts across the globe. Investors could capitalize on these commodities either by direct ownership - purchasing farmland and managing production - or through indirect methods such as buying stocks in public agricultural companies, agri-focused Real Estate Investment Trusts (REITs), or ETFs.

While the former method provides investors with more control over their investments, this avenue requires expertise in farming practices. The latter options, although lacking direct control, offer diversification without requiring in-depth agricultural knowledge.

5.2. Livestock

Like crop farming, livestock production can yield substantial returns. Livestock sector includes cattle for beef production, poultry, dairy farming, and smaller markets like goat and sheep farming. An investor can participate directly or indirectly in these markets. Direct investments generally involve purchasing a farm, while indirect methods can cover a spectrum of options such as investing in public or private companies related to the livestock industry.

5.3. Aquaculture

Aquaculture - the farming of fish, shellfish, and aquatic plants - is a relatively nascent but swiftly expanding industry with immense potential. This industry is supported by significant technological advancements. Investment opportunities range from owning and operating farms to investing in tech companies providing innovative solutions to aquaculture problems.

5.4. Agricultural Technologies

The agricultural sector is ripe for disruption and innovation, which is where AgTech enters the landscape. AgTech companies span a range from those focusing on precision farming, leveraging data science to optimize yield, to those engaged in creating new bio-engineered seeds. Investors can tap into this emerging market by buying shares in publicly traded AgTech companies or investing venture capital in promising startups.

5.5. Vertical and Urban Farming

From the window gardens of Brooklyn to the rooftop farms of Singapore, vertical and urban farming have gained significant traction in recent years. Investing in this sector might involve starting a venture or supporting startups that are redefining how we envision agriculture in cities. Sectors may involve everything from traditional vegetables to vertical mushroom farms.

5.6. Alternative Crops

Investors with a high-risk tolerance may be intrigued by the potential for huge returns associated with alternative crops. With changes in legislation and shifts in public opinion, crops such as cannabis and hemp are becoming viable commercial agricultural commodities. Investment options extend from owning farmland and producing these crops to investing in companies that process these plants into marketable products.

5.7. Commodities Trading

Agricultural commodities trading is another potential investment avenue. This is a high-risk, high-reward strategy that involves speculating on the future price movements of agricultural goods. Investors can participate in this market through commodity futures contracts or by investing in commodity-focused funds.

5.8. Farmland Investment Companies

Several companies are solely dedicated to investing in farming real estates. They operate by pooling funds from investors, purchasing, and managing agricultural land, and then distributing the profits back to the investors. Either public or private, these companies provide an enticing avenue for exposure to agriculture without direct, hands-on involvement.

5.9. Impact Investing

This approach ties the dual objectives of financial gains and creating a positive social and/or environmental impact. An example is investing in sustainable agriculture projects that reduce greenhouse gas emissions or projects that improve the economic conditions of farming communities.

Before deciding, remember that every investment involves some degree of risk. Craft a strategy that aligns with your investment goals and risk tolerance. Whether you're drawn to the familiar rhythms of traditional farming, or to the frontier landscape of vertical farming, agriculture, with its myriad opportunities, offers you avenues to reap sustainable and financial benefits. The key lies in understanding these options, making informed choices, and nurturing your investments with patience, much like a farmer with their crops.

Chapter 6. Profiting from Organic: The New Gold Standard

Over the last decade, millions of consumers around the world have begun to question the environmental and health effects of industrial-scale farming. To allay these concerns, many people have turned to organic food products, driving a boom in the organic agriculture sector. What was once a niche market is quickly becoming mainstream, offering investors an exciting opportunity for substantial returns.

6.1. The Rising Demand for Organic Products

The global organic foods market is growing at an unprecedented rate. Estimates suggest that the market is set to exceed $320 billion by 2025, representing a compound annual growth rate of nearly 17% since 2018. To meet this rising demand, the area of land used for organic farming has increased dramatically, but it still only represents about 1% of the total agricultural land worldwide. This high demand and limited supply create a potential goldmine for investors.

The driving force behind this growth is a global shift in consumer attitudes. Health-conscious consumers, particularly millennials and Gen Z, are willing to pay premium prices for organic food due to its perceived health benefits, superior taste, and lesser environmental impact. Additionally, these attitudes are becoming more widespread in emerging markets as middle-class populations grow and become more health and environment conscious.

6.2. Investment Opportunities in the Organic Sector

In the organic sector, investment opportunities are vast and varied. The most direct approach is to invest in organic farms and farming co-operatives, either by purchasing farmland and converting it to organic or by providing start-up capital to established organic farms looking to expand. However, it's worth noting that organic farming practices are inherently complex. They require significant time and resources to implement and may take several years to become profitable.

Other promising areas for investment include businesses involved in the processing, distribution, and retailing of organic goods. The aforementioned industry growth has strained existing infrastructure, sparking a demand for more processing facilities, better distribution networks, and more retail outlets specializing in organic products.

Tech-driven solutions such as organic food delivery platforms, e-commerce marketplaces for organic products, or agricultural technology companies focusing on improving the productivity and profitability of organic farming operations are also garnering significant investor interest.

Investing in the organic sector also offers opportunities to diversify across various crops, livestock, and regions. Major organic crops include cereals, oilseeds, and pulses, fruit and vegetables, spices and herbs, coffee and tea, and more. Furthermore, the demand for organic meat and dairy products is also growing, providing another promising avenue for investments.

6.3. The Profitability of Organic Farming

When it comes to the economic viability and profitability of organic versus conventional farming, the research is quite promising. While it is true that organic farming often incurs higher costs due to increased labor, the need for more specialized machinery, and longer production times, these costs are commonly offset by the premium prices organic products fetch on the market.

Several studies have compared the financial performance of organic and conventional agriculture. A meta-analysis of 55 studies found that organic farms were 22% more profitable than their conventional counterparts, despite lower yields. This profitability comes from the price premium that organic products command, along with other factors such as lower energy costs and government subsidies for sustainable farming practices.

6.4. Making Organic Investments Work for You

While organic farming is growing and profitable, it is also complex. Investors must navigate issues such as regulatory compliance, supply chain management, and market volatility. Therefore, thorough due diligence is necessary before making an investment.

First, it's crucial to gain a solid understanding of organic standards and certification processes, as they vary by region and can significantly impact an investment's profitability. Second, understanding the organic market and its trends, from consumer demand to supply chain dynamics, is equally important. Third, it's beneficial to assemble a team or work with consultants who have expertise in organic farming and agribusiness.

Finally, consider diversifying. As with all investment, spreading capital across different projects, geographic regions, and types of organic crops or livestock can reduce risk and increase potential returns.

6.5. The Future of Organic Investments

The growth of the organic sector is set to continue, spurred on by rising consumer awareness about climate change and the environmental impact of agriculture. As more people turn towards sustainable lifestyle and dietary choices, organic products will keep gaining market share. On the supply-side, technological advancements are making organic farming more efficient and productive, further boosting its profitability.

Investors who position themselves in this sector now stand to profit handsomely in the coming years. As the gold standard in sustainable agriculture, investing in the organic movement presents a unique opportunity to generate both financial returns and a positive impact on the planet. Consider it an invitation to plant the seeds for a buoyant future in a sector that upholds the health of the earth and its inhabitants - truly a win-win proposition.

Chapter 7. Tech-driven Agriculture: The Future is Now

Farmers have sown the seeds and tilled the fields for centuries, intrinsically tying their livelihood to the land. But in the 21st century, the farmer's traditional toolbox has evolved, and alongside the plow and the tractor, there's now a place for drones, artificial intelligence (AI), and blockchain technologies. Today, agricultural practices are closely wedded to these technological advancements, reshaping farming's future and making agriculture an exciting and valuable investment opportunity.

7.1. A Birds-Eye View: Drones in Agriculture

Unmanned aerial vehicles, better known as drones, have been vital game-changers within the agricultural sector. These winged devices can monitor crop growth with pinpoint accuracy, empowering farmers to maximize yields and reduce waste. Employing aerial imagery and remote sensing capabilities, drones offer real-time field data, enabling early detection of crop diseases, pest attacks, and hydration levels.

Such precision farming leads to higher productivity and cost-efficiency. Farmers can deploy resources tactically, applying fertilizers and pesticides only where required, which also bears environmental benefits. Therefore, investing in drone technology holds promising returns both financially and environmentally.

7.2. Artificial Intelligence: A Rich Harvest of Data

AI, with its capacity to unravel complex patterns and make intelligent predictions, has ushered in a new era of data-driven farming. An AI model, when fed data from images, weather patterns, soil analysis, and historical crop yield, can infer the optimal time to sow seeds, predict pest attacks, and even forecast yields with remarkable accuracy.

AI-powered robotic technology platforms add another layer of sophistication. They can perform tedious tasks such as weeding and fruit picking at a much faster pace and lower cost than human labor. These advancements allow farmers to produce more at reduced expenses, leading to higher profitability, depicting AI technology as an investment worth cultivating.

7.3. The Application of IoT in Agriculture

The Internet of Things (IoT) technology incorporates a network of sensors, drones, and GPS systems to collect real-time data and monitor the health of farmlands. IoT devices measure factors like soil moisture, light intensity, temperature, and nutrient levels, transmitting this data to farmers or AI systems for analysis.

Within this context, smart irrigation systems have seen widespread use. These systems utilize precise soil moisture measurements to automate irrigation schedules, ensuring water is used judiciously. IoT integration leads to a heightened production capacity with minimized risks, making it an enticing area for investors in technology-savvy agriculture space.

7.4. Blockchain: Bringing Transparency to Supply Chains

In an industry where transparency and traceability are crucial, blockchain technology has found a fitting application. Blockchain, a decentralized ledger, allows all transactions to be recorded and tracked securely, promising enhanced transparency and reduced fraud risk.

From the farm to the consumer's table, each product's complete journey can be traced, establishing trust in the produce's quality and origin. This transparency appealed to conscious consumers demanding sustainable produce, simultaneously providing farmers with a sales boost. Investing in blockchain infrastructure for agriculture can deliver substantial returns, riding the wave of a demand-driven market.

7.5. Biotechnology: Engineering Superior Crop Varieties

Biotechnology, through genetic modification and gene editing, has been instrumental in devising crop varieties with desirable traits, such as higher nutrient content, improved taste, resistance to pests, or tolerance to harsh climate conditions. Such enhancements not only increase crop yields but also extend geographic boundaries for farming certain crops.

While public sentiments on genetically modified organisms (GMOs) can be polarized, the potential for biotech in improving food security and sustainability cannot be overlooked. Investment in biotech provides an opportunistic avenue to engage with a technology poised to shape agriculture's future.

Moving beyond the traditional perception of farming, it's clear that technology is revolutionizing the agricultural industry. As these innovations continue to unfold, they present fertile ground for investors seeking sustainable and rewarding returns. In this age of digital transformation, it's not an overstatement to say that the future of agriculture is now; the time has come to sow the seeds of tomorrow.

Chapter 8. Risk Mitigation Strategies in Agro-Investing

Understanding the dynamics of agriculture and related risk elements is paramount for any investor looking to venture into this burgeoning sector. The risks in agricultural investments can be categorized broadly into production risks, market risks, institutional risks, personal risks, and financial risks. It is essential to comprehend these factors intimately and to extrapolate effective mitigation strategies to maximize the dividend potential for your investments.

8.1. Production risks

Weather events compared to other industries uniquely complicate production risks in agriculture; these include floods, drought, hail, frost, pests, and diseases, all capable of severely hampering agricultural yield.

Mitigation strategies for production risks include:

1. Opting for agricultural insurance: This can provide a safety net for investments in case of unforeseen weather events or pest infestations. There are several agricultural insurance products available, such as multi-peril crop insurance and crop-revenue insurance.

2. Diversifying agricultural production: A diversified farm is less likely to suffer devastating losses from any single event. This means not only planting a variety of crops but potentially also including complementary production such as livestock.

3. Investing in technology: Innovations in agriculture, such as predictive AI for weather events and biotechnology for disease resistance, can offer improved resilience against these types of risks.

8.2. Market Risks

Market risks are the price variations for both inputs (seeds, fertilizers, water, etc.) and outputs (grains, fruits, vegetables, livestock, etc.).

Mitigation strategies for market risks include:

1. Forward contracts: These are agreements to sell or buy commodities at a future date at a predetermined price, offering protections from price variations.
2. Developing value-added products: By enhancing your agricultural produce, you not only diversify your revenue streams but also reduce the impact of market price fluctuations on raw products.
3. Geographic diversification: This tactic can help counter the impact of local market demand-supply imbalances by selling in several markets.

8.3. Institutional Risks

Institutional risks include regulatory changes in tariff and trade policies, environmental regulations, land reforms, and taxation.

Mitigation strategies for institutional risks include:

1. Legal due diligence: Understand the legal terrain of your agricultural venture and ensure all regulations and laws are adhered to.
2. Hiring consultants or advisors with local expertise: Specialists can help navigate policy changes and regulatory norms, ensuring business continuity.

8.4. Personal Risks

Personal risks are tied to an individual or a company's capacities and can include issues like health emergencies, skill gaps, labor shortages, or succession planning challenges.

Mitigation strategies for personal risks include:

1. Developing a robust succession plan: This can ensure business continuity in the face of personal challenges.

2. Adequate health and work insurance: Providing insurance for workers can ensure minimal disruptions due to health emergencies.

3. Education and skill development programs: Upskilling the workforce can patch potential skill gaps that might impact farming operations.

8.5. Financial Risks

Financial risks include variations in interest rates, access to credit, and managing cash flow effectively.

Mitigation strategies for financial risks include:

1. Building strong relationships with multiple lenders: This can ensure continued access to credit at competitive rates.

2. Effective cash flow management: Regularly updating financial projections and performance indicators aid in managing cash flow.

3. Contingency planning: Having a financial buffer and contingency plans in place is critical in managing unexpected events.

Investing in agriculture, just like any other venture, requires a balanced and well-thought-out strategy. Risk mitigation is a crucial aspect of this strategy. Despite being a sector fraught with unique challenges, smart and calculated measures can help one harvest the benefits while avoiding the pitfalls. Understanding the terrain and weathering the storms are all part of the route to eventual success in the arena of agricultural investing.

Chapter 9. Sustainable Agriculture: Greening Your Portfolio

The world is catching on to the merits of sustainable agriculture, recognizing its role not only in food security but also in combating climate change and mitigating its impacts. Sustainable agriculture represents a potent investment strategy for a green portfolio, with various aspects that make it an attractive, forward-looking, and a decidedly secure bet.

9.1. The Why: Understanding the Need for Sustainable Practices

The reasons to transition to sustainable agriculture are manifold. Globally, agriculture contributes nearly a quarter of total greenhouse gas emissions, making it a major contributor to climate change. Further, traditional farming methods often involve practices that degrade the soil, pollute water, and diminish biodiversity. Sustainable agriculture stands as an antidote to these problems.

There's also an economic incentive. The growing demand for sustainably grown, organic food products presents a lucrative market opportunity. By the United Nations' estimates, the global organic food market is set to reach $323.56 billion by 2024.

9.2. The How: Promoting Sustainability in Agriculture

Sustainable agriculture involves a gamut of practices aimed at minimizing environmental harms while meeting humanity's food and fiber needs. These practices include organic farming, permaculture, agroforestry, crop rotation, and conservation tillage. Each of these represents a potential investment opportunity.

- **Organic Farming:** Organic farming refrains from using synthetic fertilizers and pesticides. Instead, it focuses on practices like crop rotation, green manure, compost, and biological pest control, significantly reducing its environmental footprint.

- **Permaculture:** It is a holistic approach that seeks to design agricultural systems mimicking natural ecosystems. Investments can be directed towards educational and training initiatives, fostering permaculture as a mainstream practice.

- **Agroforestry:** This practice integrates trees into crop and livestock fields, improving biodiversity and soil health and sequestering carbon.

- **Crop Rotation and Conservation Tillage:** These practices reduce soil erosion and improve soil fertility, promoting long-term productivity and resilience against climatic fluctuations.

9.3. Investment Avenues: Where to Put Your Money

Several investment avenues exist for channels your capital towards sustainable agriculture.

- **Farmland Funds:** These funds directly invest in sustainable agricultural lands, leasing them to farmers, or operating the farms themselves. This is an excellent way of gaining exposure to the sector.

- **AgTech Companies:** Companies that develop advanced farming technologies like precision agriculture, automated irrigation systems, or ag-tech platforms fostering smarter farming practices are ripe for investments.

- **Sustainable Livestock and Aquaculture Operations:** Firms that adopt low-impact, humane livestock practices and ecologically enhancing aquaculture methods represent sound investment options.

- **Value-added Product Companies:** Investing in companies that produce value-added sustainable products like organic food items or biodegradable materials also offers substantial returns.

9.4. Risks and Challenges: The Other Side of the Coin

Sustainable agriculture is not without its challenges. The transition from traditional to sustainable farming can be expensive and require training. Productivity can also decrease in the short term. Further, if climate change continues unabated, even sustainably managed soils and systems may suffer.

However, as with any investment, informed decisions are key. Thorough due diligence, understanding the business model and management structure, recognizing market trends, and regulatory considerations can aid in risk management and investment success.

9.5. The Road Ahead: Future Of Sustainable Investments in Agriculture

Growing awareness of the climate crisis, increasing investor interest in Environmental, Social, and Governance (ESG) factors, and the rising demand for organic food show that inclusion of sustainable agriculture in an investment portfolio is a future-proof strategy.

Moreover, policies favoring sustainable agriculture, innovations in AgTech, and the growing adoption of sustainable farming practices make the sector an increasingly compelling option. As more financial instruments geared towards sustainable agriculture come into existence, the opportunities to invest and generate substantial returns will continue to broaden.

Building a green portfolio through investment in sustainable agriculture not only promises attractive returns but also allows you to contribute to a healthier planet. Going forward, we anticipate seeing an influx of investments flowing into sustainable agriculture, becoming a cornerstone for progressive wealth creation, financial stability, and ecological resilience.

Chapter 10. Global Insights: Investing in International Agriculture

Recent years have experienced a dramatic shift in global investment paradigms as the agricultural sector began receiving increasing attention from a diverse range of investors. Individuals, corporations, and venture capitalists, now more than ever, are keen to tap into the wealth-building potential offered by the agricultural sector, not only referred to the traditional farming techniques, but also considering advancements in technology, sustainability, and agricultural innovation on a global scale.

10.1. Global Market Overview

To understand the compelling prospects of investing in international agriculture, it's essential to get an insightful overview of the global market. The global demand for food is expected to increase by 70% by 2050, according to the Food and Agriculture Organization of the United Nations. Rapid urbanization and population growth, particularly in developing economies, are driving this demand. As global food production strains under increasing environmental pressures, innovative agricultural technologies and practices present attractive investment avenues.

As an asset class, agriculture is resilient to economic downturns. According to a Food and Agricultural Policy Research Institute report, global agricultural trade has steadily increased between 2001 and 2020, despite fluctuating economic conditions. Simultaneously, increasing demands on water, land, and energy resources underline the urgency for sustainable innovations in the sector, which investors can potentially profit from.

10.2. Understanding Investment Opportunities

Investment prospects in international agriculture are as diverse as the sector itself. The opportunities range from traditional farming and agriculture to agri-tech startups pioneering the fields of precision farming, vertical farming, or aquaponics.

Investment in export-oriented markets such as Brazil, Argentina, and the United States offer opportunities in large-scale farming for soybeans, corn, and wheat. As global demand for these commodities increase, investors may benefit from economies of scale and favorable export policies.

Emerging economies, particularly in sub-Saharan Africa and Southeast Asia, offer unique investment opportunities in cash crops like cacao, coffee, or tea. Despite challenges such as lack of infrastructural development and political instability, the potential rewards can be significant, particularly when the investment enhances local sustainability and inclusivity.

10.3. Technological Innovations in Agriculture

Technological advancements are revolutionizing global agriculture. They provide enticing avenues for venture capital investments, particularly in biotech firms involved in developing new crop varieties or agri-tech startups pioneering precision and vertical farming.

Precision farming uses technologies like IoT, GPS, and AI to optimize crop yields and resource utilization. Startups in this field offer investment opportunities that can yield high returns as demand for tech-driven farming increases.

Vertical farming, an innovative method of producing food in vertically stacked layers or inclined surfaces within controlled environments, is gaining traction in urban areas. Investing in startups that design, build, and operate vertical farms, particularly in areas with high population densities and limited arable land, may yield promising returns.

Further, investments in firms working to develop climate-resistant crop strains or innovative, sustainable farming methodologies could deliver significant dividends, while combating the global challenge of climate change.

10.4. Risks and Mitigation

Investing in international agriculture is not without risks. Global market dynamics, geopolitical tensions, changing climatic conditions, and potential pest invasions are a few of the many risks that must be accounted for and managed.

Mitigation strategies include diversification across different agricultural commodities and regions, ensuring investments align with appropriate international standards, and leveraging agricultural insurance products. Further, investment choices should reflect the balance between potential returns and economic, environmental, and social sustainability.

10.5. Crafting a Strategic Investment Portfolio

Formulating an investment portfolio in international agriculture would require careful analysis of global trends, regional characteristics, diverse agricultural products, and technological trends. It's recommended to diversify investments across traditional farming, agri-tech startups, and innovative agri-food firms. It's also beneficial to include both developed and emerging economies, each presenting unique risk-to-reward ratios.

Portfolio balancing should also account for long-term geopolitical and socio-economic trends. For instance, Africa's rapidly growing youth population and Asia's urbanization trend might influence the choice of investments.

10.6. Final Thoughts

In conclusion, the international agricultural sector holds impressive wealth-building potential. Its resilience to economic downturns, the global push for sustainability, and the promise of technological innovations collectively present exciting opportunities for both novice and experienced investors. Crafting a carefully diversified, balanced portfolio that reflects the investor's risk appetite, investment horizon, and ethical considerations can yield healthy dividends while contributing positively to global sustainability goals.

This journey into international agricultural investments is varied, offering a mix of traditional and innovative approaches. But one thing is certain - the rewards for patient and discerning investors can be substantial, both financially and in terms of contributing to the world's need for sustainable and efficient food production systems.

Chapter 11. The Future of Agricultural Investment: Trends and Predictions

In the recent past, agricultural investments have transcended the traditional boundaries of crop production and livestock rearing, morphing into a sophisticated playing field where technology, social awareness, and economic prowess converge. Let's delve into key trends that signify the future of this thriving sector.

11.1. Sustainable and Organic Farming: A Modern Gold Rush

From a niche market to a mainstream one, the surge in consumer demand for organic food has led to an impressive escalation in organic farming. As per the Research Institute of Organic Agriculture (FiBL), global organic food sales reached almost $100 billion in 2018, showcasing an excellent avenue for potential investors. Estimates also suggest that the global organic food market is projected to grow at a five-year CAGR of about 10%, surpassing the growth rate of the overall food market, highlighting the significant investment potential.

Studies prove that consumers are willing to pay a premium for organic commodities, due to the perceived health and environmental benefits. Thus, an investment in this area seems promising for substantial returns. On the sustainability front, investing in eco-friendly practices like rainwater harvesting, permaculture, or hydroponics could yield long-term benefits, not just financially, but also by contributing to the broader global initiative of climate change mitigation.

11.2. AgriTech: The New Catalyst for Growth

Agricultural technology or AgriTech has risen to prominence in recent years, driven by the need to feed a growing global population effectively and sustainably. AgriTech encompasses various facets ranging from biotechnology and machine learning to satellite imagery and automation, all aimed at boosting crop productivity, reducing waste, and creating resilient food systems.

Looking forward, the AgriTech sector is set for monumental growth. According to data from AgFunder, global investments in AgriTech startups reached $19.8 billion across 1938 deals in 2019, depicting a significant upswing. Venture capitalists, recognizing the potential of AgriTech, are increasingly funding startups engaged in innovative farming technologies, creating satisfying returns on their investments.

Innovation in AgriTech, such as automated irrigation systems, precision farming, and vertical farming, augur well for investors. Precision farming, for example, leverages IoT sensors and big data to enhance crop yields and allow more efficient use of resources, making it a tempting prospect for savvy investors.

11.3. Agricultural Real Estate: A Tangible Asset

Agricultural real estate, denoting land used for farming operations, has always been enticing for those seeking solid, tangible investments. Beyond the scope of traditional farmland investing, farmland real estate investment trusts (REITs) or crowd-funded investments platforms are emerging as accessible alternatives for individual investors who may not have the means to directly own agricultural property.

Historically, farmland values have shown less volatility compared to commercial real estate and equities, making them a viable option for diversification. Historically an asset class linked to elitist investors, the democratization of this field via REITs and crowd-funded platforms widens the opportunity base.

Agricultural real estate, besides generating capital appreciation, can accrue income from farming operations, giving it a dual-income nature. According to the USDA, average U.S farmland values rose from about $1,100 per acre in 2000 to $3,160 in 2020, demonstrating a steady upward trajectory.

11.4. Investing in Livestock

With the global populace burgeoning and developing countries witnessing increased meat consumption due to higher disposable incomes, the livestock sector will likely maintain its relevance for the foreseeable future. As per a report by the FAO, consumption of meat is projected to increase by nearly 1% per year until 2030. Consequently, investments in livestock, whether in enhancing feed efficiency, animal genetic development, or healthier livestock rearing practices, are ripe for growth.

Alternative proteins, such as lab-grown meat or plant-based substitutes, are also witnessing robust demand as consumers increasingly adopt flexitarian diets. Investments in this innovative segment, though nascent, are evidencing robust returns.

11.5. Climate Smart Agriculture

Climate smart agriculture (CSA), a combination of sustainable production methods and innovative technology, is aimed at building resilience against the effects of climate change. This approach includes novel farming techniques like conservation agriculture, agroforestry, and climate-smart livestock management.

Investing in companies that align with CSA practices or technologies enabling these methodologies could result in both financial and environmental returns. With global climate change agreements spotlighting the need to adapt agriculture for a warmer world, the importance of CSA, and thus the potential for substantial returns on investments within this sector, is undoubted.

In closing, agriculture as an investment avenue is witnessing a dramatic redefinition, driven by advances in technology and heightened environmental and social consciousness. Traditional fields of agriculture like livestock rearing or organic farming are being reshaped by the influx of new technologies and innovation, while rising trends like AgriTech and smart farming promise sustainable and lucrative future investment opportunities. As we navigate through the 21st century, it seems clear that agriculture will not only continue to provide sustenance but also solid, dependable investment returns.

www.ingramcontent.com/pod-product-compliance
Lightning Source LLC
Chambersburg PA
CBHW062305290526
45794CB00006B/2707